Dear Congress,

Voices of American Children
Currently Being Abused By
Conversion Therapy

Dear Congress,

Voices of American Children Currently Being Abused By **Conversion Therapy**

Sincerely,

Vellah Jones & the Children's Committee

Legacy Projects

To the beautiful sum,
from the depths of truth

. . .

CONTENTS

A Note from the Author

Dear Readers,

I wrote this book for America. Please understand that it may be hard to read, but you must push through. When you want to put it down, just keep pushing. Children are being abused & coerced into suicide in America, and they need you to pay attention.

This book addresses conversion therapy practices on minors, which is child abuse, and attempts to change the sexual orientation or gender identity of an individual. This book shares experiences of children who were encouraged to attempt suicide by state licensed mental health professionals because of their sexual orientation or gender identity. Regardless of your gender identity, sexual orientation, race or religion your voice is important to ensure the well-being of every American. Remember, your awareness is important.

First read; then act.

From the future, I thank you for reading this,

VELLAH JONES

●

Please Note: Names and identifying information of the victims included here have been altered to protect their privacy. In some cases, the letters represent a composite of victims' stories. I chose this format to both help disguise the identities of victims and to allow me to include information about conversion therapy. This book is for, and from, all those who contributed to its creation in the hopes of providing them a voice for their stories, including myself, and enacting legislative change. The composite of stories are actual instances of life experiences with conversion therapy on minors.

1

Did You Arrive in a Drawer or by Bassinet?

Did You Arrive in a Drawer or by Bassinet?

Do you bear red in your soul?
I tell the tale of unknowing darkness,
of the wonder to grow old on the other side.
I grew up behind the lens, somewhere between blind and all seeing.
Now, a shadow in the open, I squint from the colors,
which pierce my eyes.

I tell the tale of a beautiful ugly.

The thing about being delivered in a drawer, and not a bassinet,
is you arrive to ride the tracks and not the wind.
To grow up on the tracks is to be nurtured from the water, which
rests inside the stones.
It is to know the bees nestled inside the pollen,
but not the softness of yellow nectar.

When you arrive in a drawer you know not the comfort of
cushion, but the love of knit. From the track comes knowing that
at some point on the path, flood and fire will rip the ground apart,
as will the lightning and wind upon the feathers in flight.

From the tracks, comes the comfort of the breeze while you dangle
your feet above steel blades. From the tracks, comes knowing how
to wave at the foot travelers to pass the time, and knowing what
foot travelers do and look like, but not to know travel by foot.

The thing about arriving in a drawer, and not a bassinet, is that
you know what it is like to know a glimpse. The thing about
arriving in a drawer and not a bassinet is the readers of black
and white are not mindful of the consequences of reading fairytales
to little girls.

At the tracks change, a traveler boards and scans the passengers, before softly taking the seat next to mine. The shapeless clouds in the distance whizz by before the traveler's hand reaches to mine to fill it with an apple and a ripe tomato.

"Children on the tracks should never ride alone," the traveler whispers, and proceeds to talk of the complexities of the grapevine.

After the one of many talents softy speaks the truth of the power of a vine's connectivity, a look of sorrow falls from the traveler's eyes to the letter grading between the fingertips.

"Why have you not opened your letter?" the girl asks.
"I fear it is the fears of my brother," the gentle person says, "who I cannot calm."

"What hurts him?"
"The same thing which pains me—the teachings gone wrong, and the will of the person standing next to us to bide them."

"May I read your letter?" the girl asks.
"No," the traveler initially insists, and pulls out a box of crayons and requests she pick one. The girl analyzes the colors, then the traveler, and turns to the window.

"But I am love," she says.
"What is your name?" the genuine traveler asks.
"I am Willow," she says, "and you are the Keeper of the Colors."

With a fond smile, the traveler hands the girl a pack of colored pencils and points to the triangular window, which is filled with clouds from storybooks, just for her.

"A present for you," the magical person says, just before leaving to read the letter.
Dearest Sister and Brother,

They do not think I will come to the mist.
They fear I will rest inside these chains forever.
One chain for another is the cruelty which awaits me,
as I know my fate is to trade my silence only for the captivity of an eternal whisper.

Whisper I will to my daughter in the rock:
Ignorance and cruelty sleep at the end of the hall.
The locks on your doors are a farce,
and cannot keep out the color blind.
The privileged rest just two doors down, and not even their offspring are safe from their chosen ignorance.

Do not be fooled with distractions in the form
questioning nature versus nurture,
for these are the weapons of diamonds,
used to saw down the willow trees in the inner yard that the ignorant would rather not see.

Their proclamation of love, in spite of your rainbow threads,
is the weight upon my soul,
as I know the sound of this truth is before you.
And with its surfaced echo the world will abide by,
and watch as a piece of innocence dies.

As I looked at my daughter's reflection, I could not speak, as the knowledge of her naïveté showed me the serpent once more.

I bellow in anger:
"Your laws are weak to the under-current of hate

which murder our children by their own hands!"

In rage, I teach my children to roar:
"You, the privileged, with your peace of mind, are color blind!
For I choose education over ignorance, and you, the privileged with
your peace of mind, choose to poison a blank canvas with
ignorance over education!"

In rage, my daughter roars:
Do you see the reflection before you?
Do you see the shreds of injustice that stare back at you?
Your golden stem nurtures the repulsion,
which is your looking glass.

Hold tight, as the garden doors turn to show you the calligraphy
burned upon your forehead.
Bear down, as the salted sandpaper's lesion shine in the polished
metal, which distorts you.
Look up, as the coeval glass echoes the blood tracks,
which fall from the scented gapes to taint your lips.
Breath deep, as the pier winds roar through your lungs,
cutting your vocal chords as they douse your denial.
Soar not, as the beam's reflection deadens the iris in your eyes.

A child once you sat and gazed upon the mommy's mirror, and
took it for thine own.

Now you stand, your thorny grasp upon my pulse,
You now the passer of the hand glass.
But weak I am not like thee,
as I throw your putrid parody back into the sea.

I love you.

Child Abuse Infects America

Child abuse is widespread and can occur in any cultural, ethnic, or income group. It can be physical, emotional, verbal, or sexual, and can also result from neglect. Abuse can cause serious injury and death.

Physical abuse involves non-accidental harm. Verbal abuse involves harm by belittling or the threat of physical or sexual acts. Emotional trauma can result from several different forms of abuse.

Approximately five children die every day because of child abuse. Ninety percent of child sexual abuse victims know the perpetrator, while 68 percent are abused by a family member. Every year 2.9 million cases of child abuse are reported in the U.S. About 80 percent of 21-year-olds who were abused as children met criteria for at least one psychological disorder.

Child sexual abuse is the deliberate exposure to sexual activity that the child cannot comprehend or consent to. This includes inappropriate touching, intercourse, exhibitionism, and exposure to pornography.

Child neglect occurs when necessities of life are not provided, either intentionally or with reckless disregard. This includes withholding food, clothing, or shelter. Emotional neglect includes withholding love or comfort or affection.

Sources: Susanne Babel, "The Lingering Trauma of Child Abuse," *Psychology Today*, April 24, 2011, www.psychologytoday.com/us/blog/somatic-psychology/201104/the-lingering-trauma-child-abuse; "11 Facts About Child Abuse," Dosomthing.org, n.d., https://www.dosomething.org/us/facts/11-facts-about-child-abuse.

FROM: Child victim Of conversion therapy
TO: P.A. State Legislature, U.S. Congress

May 11, 2018

Dear Elected Officials,

I write to you in desperation. I write to you hoping that in your heart you know you have a responsibility to protect the youth of America from child abuse and suicide. I write to you from the depths of anguish, which began with the injustices imposed upon me at the hands of licensed mental health professionals.

I beseech you. Please read this letter and react with knowledge and discernment. Please choose education over ignorance and save the future of this country by providing a truth we do not yet know. You can do this by providing our youth with assurance that our government is here to protect American children from harm.

Incidence of licensed mental health professionals' using conversion therapy techniques on American minors, in an effort to change their sexual orientation or gender identity, is rising and has now reached levels in the hundreds of thousands. Damages resulting from these techniques are negatively impacting the physical, psychological and emotional well-being of children at a detrimental rate and in a significant amount of cases ends in child suicide, homelessness, addiction or worse.

Conversion therapy is a compilation of "therapeutic" techniques that have been determined to be unfounded and ineffective by the APA, Centers for Disease Control, WHO and the Child Abuse Prevention and Treatment Act.

Conversion therapy also often includes the types of psychological and physical abuse familiar to abused children not subjected to conversion therapy. Types of child abuse used in conversion therapy on minors include, but are not limited to:

➢ Coercing suicide and suicidal role play in an effort to encourage the act of suicide

➢ Forced exposure to heterosexual behavior in visual, verbal and actual forms

➢ Various forms of corporal punishment including, but not limited to: hitting, slapping, punching, burning, poking and pinching

➢ Coercing self-harm including snapping a rubber band around the left wrist

➢ Verbal abuse including name calling and negative labeling

➢ Neglect including deliberately with holding physical and verbal affection necessary for adequate development

➢ Electro shock therapy

➢ Coercing self-mutilation in the form of using a needle to damage and peel off one's skin

➢ Hypnosis in an effort to brain wash

➢ The use of drugs to induce incoherence and immobilization

➢ Orgasmic reconditioning

I am confused as to why it is considered incomprehensible to coerce my straight brother to kill himself, but for me it is acceptable in the eyes of the law?

My experience was at one of the top high schools on the east coast, and the love I received from my teachers and principals is to be commended.

My nightmare began when I came home from first grade and told my mom that I thought girls were beautiful. I was made to swear I wasn't a lesbian, even though I didn't know what that even was.

That is when the mental manipulation began.

It was just a few years after that when I was told that I had to leave the house and go live on the streets because I thought girls were pretty.

I promised and pleaded that I was not a lesbian, and I begged to stay home. I was told I had to prove it. My mother sat me on the couch with her brother and let him sexually abuse me. She was given guidance by a trained professional therapist that if children are exposed to heterosexual behavior when they are young, they will become heterosexual. I had to tell my mother and grandmother that I liked it with my uncle. I remember saying again and again how much I liked it; and pleading with all of them that I was not gay, and begging them to let me stay home. I remember thinking how much I loved my sister, and that I couldn't live without her, and I had to stay because I loved her so much.

I weighed my options. Either go live on the streets and end up in a foster home, where I feared it would be just as bad, or stay in this house of horror where at least I knew I had my sister.

I did not speak a single word that entire summer.

That is when I went into a state of shock. I learned to take the beatings and bear the verbal hate spewed upon me by my mom. I had no choice.

One of the biggest mistakes people make about this whole conversion therapy thing is thinking that all of us are sent away from home for "treatment." But for me, and a lot of other kids, it happens at home, and the therapists are not a plane ride away, but rather an instructional phone call or grim car ride away.

I guess that's why I'm sharing my story. Because you need to know it is happening in this town, in the homes you drive by every day. That's where conversion therapy takes place.

The therapists are a terror not even the most horrid of words could bring to justice. Their hypnosis left me totally disconnected from people. Their drugs left me incoherent, and their attempts at cognitive and behavioral therapy, using physical, psychological, and mental manipulation techniques, have done, I fear, irreparable damage.

What weighs me down with unspeakable sorrow is being told by my parents, family members, and doctors that I should kill myself because I am a demon, as if we're on some TV show about zombies or something. At first, I asked myself, "Are they for real?" I quickly learned that they are definitely for real.

They taught me how to do it, you know. They made me visualize putting a gun to my head and pulling the trigger. They had me choose the bridge they hope I will jump from some day.

I remember being forced to tell them what I think it will feel like when I hit the water. A child in sixth grade being forced to play out her own suicide for mental health professionals and her family is a life sentence of mental torture that never goes away.

For now, I will gaze out the windows and wonder what life is still left. I will remember the gymnasium and appreciate the attention given to the polished floors and prideful students. And all the while, I will be wondering what awaits me.

Legislators of Justice, I ask you to look at your own children and consider all the children you walk by on the street.

I am asking you to think about all of these children. Can you honestly tell yourself that conversion therapy techniques imposed upon minors is not child abuse, or worse?

If you have done this, I can only hope at the time that you did not know. But, now you know.

I am asking you to choose education over ignorance.

I am asking you to do whatever you can to stop mental health professionals who are licensed in the state of Pennsylvania from doing harm to the children in your communities by practicing conversion therapy intended to change their sexual orientation or gender identity.

It is time to implement laws which prohibit Pennsylvania licensed mental health professionals from practicing conversion therapy on minors intended to change their sexual orientation or gender identity. It is time to stop permitting the coercion of child suicide in Pennsylvania. I was just a child. They are just children.

Sincerely,
Your Very Loving Daughter

2

The Dream Of America

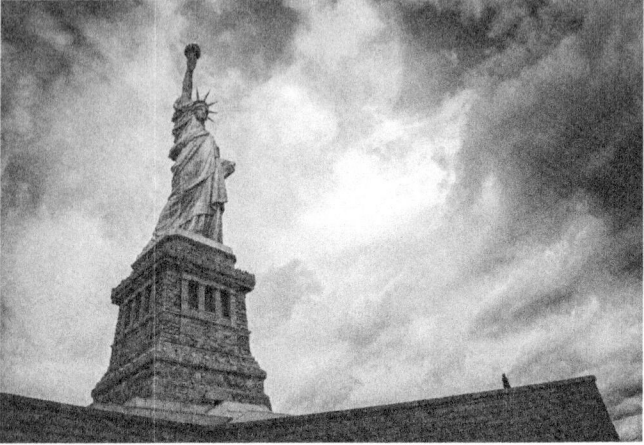

The Dream Of America

*There is a truth to be told. There is a whisper, which is really a
yell.
We live in a world driven by conformity and fear.
The conversion of America is a story, which lives in the houses
that hold the children of then and now, and are built on the
foundation of abide to institutions over family.*

*There is a mirror, which reflects the truths about bide,
in the home, in the community, and in our country.
You see, the beauty of bide is that it can birth true glory,
but when it is misused as a current behind a force of conversion
against nature, it can become a true threat to humankind.*

*I dare to write the truth about our experiences of those who abide,
Bide…and how their teachings create boldness or blindness.
I dare to write the truth of childhood experiences of
institutionalized ignorance within a society that breeds darkness
for the different.*

*Listen to the magnificence of the Arts and their song,
which sing not the notes of the American Dream,
but of the Dream of America…a wish that a country will not
become any more divided than it already is, bound by the fear of
evolvement, fueled by teachings of a singular existence, and driven
by the radical conversion of innocence and the sale of white picket
fences. I dare to write the hopes of the Arts to create a melting pot
of culture.*

*I write to acknowledge the ingredients, which make up this
Master Chef's concoction of Country and Culture. For it is the
corruption of dreams which binds us to the delusion of justice for
all, and gives fuel to the stereotypes, which have become the barbed*

wire's weave across our land and the murders of now and then.

No matter what, we must all remember,
There is no you and I; there is only us.
And maybe, just for a little while,
We should start living the Dream of America.

WHO Largely Ignored

Despite organizations like WHO, the World Health Organization, and the efforts of local, state and federal agencies, child abuse of all kinds is often overlooked and under-estimated by legislators who do not do the work to protect our nation's children.

According to Voices for Children, a private, non-profit organization, each state is responsible for establishing its own definitions of child abuse and neglect that meet federal minimum standards. Most definitions include the following:

1. Neglect is failure to provide for a child's basic needs.

2. Physical abuse is a result of hitting, kicking, shaking, burning, or otherwise harming a child.

3. Sexual abuse is a situation in which a child is used for sexual gratification, including indecent exposure, fondling, rape, exploitation through prostitution, or the production of pornographic materials.

4. Emotional abuse is a pattern of behavior that impairs a child's emotional development or sense of self-worth, including criticism, threats, and rejection.

Local counties, police departments, and social services are not always up to the task, leaving many children to slip through the cracks, where they must fend for themselves without adequate support, let alone loving kindness. One of the largest groups of children to fall into this category are those who have been victimized by conversion therapy.

Source: "Child Abuse Statistics & Resources," Voices for Children, n.d., https://www.speakupnow.org/child-abuse-statistics-resources/.

FROM: Child Victim Of conversion therapy
TO: Ohio State Legislature, U.S. Congress

August 4, 2017

Dear Elected Officials,

Growing up around these parts could have been worse, I suppose. After all, I had it pretty good compared to the kids on the other side of town. I'm not one of the "free lunch" kids, or one of the guys who pretend they don't know Spanish in class but speak it fluently at home.

All of the kids made it easier for me to blend in, as if maybe the teachers won't be able to see the pain among the sea of desperate hope and helplessness.

I know it's not their fault because their hands are tied. The teachers may have seen what went on, but the law won't allow them to intervene on my behalf. It's not like they could go to social services and say, "This child is being abused," especially when our state law permits this abuse.

That is why I agreed to write this letter. I am relieved because I understand what's going on now. But when I was in elementary school and didn't understand what was happening, it really twisted me in the head.

My parents took me to a therapist sometime during 4th grade. They said they were going to help me with "social problems." Whenever I asked them to explain, they literally ignored me and kept telling me I was a bad, messed up kid, but they never told me why.

Talk about mind games. That's when my dad really started to hate my guts. It just happened overnight, as if he got a list of what to do from the therapists on how to act, what to do with his face, and when to acknowledge me, or not.

The therapists told me that my parents would be doing things at home and in public to help keep me in line with "appropriate social behavior." I remember them saying that and thinking, what does "appropriate" mean? They said there was good behavior and bad behavior and when I was a bad boy and did things that made me an evil and sick person, my parents were going to do things that would punish me, because I needed it to ensure that I didn't go to jail or to hell. I said okay only because I was terrified of jail and hell, so I said okay because I had no other choice.

It started with them ignoring me when I talked. My dad would storm out of the room and slam the door as hard as he could whenever I talked. My mom mostly yelled and pulled me really hard and told me I was a disgusting person whenever I hummed the music from music class.

I wasn't allowed to listen to music at home, so music class in school always sent me home singing. It's weird when you sit in class and are taught about great musicians, such as Beethoven and Pavarotti, but when you go home you are given a beating for humming the beautiful.

The beatings started when my dad walked in on me one day while I was playing with my mom's red shoes.

Fourth grade was a blur.

My dad came right up behind me and punched me as hard as he could right between the shoulder blades.

It's funny the things you notice when you're face down on the ground. It wasn't the pain that caught me off guard. It was the baseboards. I just remember noticing how clean the baseboards were and thinking, I hope I don't blow any dust onto the baseboards, or accidentally spit on them or something. Cleaning the baseboards is one of my chores, and the last thing I want to do is give my mom another reason to rant like the world is ending.

Between the blades is my dad's place of choice.

If we are in public and he doesn't like what I am doing he grabs the top of my shoulder and digs his fingers right into my blades. Most of the time it's because he doesn't like how I am standing or what I am looking at. If he pinches me when we are out in public, I always dread getting into the car, because I know what is coming.

"You make me look like such an idiot!" he says. "You're disgusting! I'm so embarrassed."

It goes one of two ways when we get home. Either I'm inspecting baseboards, or my mom, brother, sister, and dad just give me the silent treatment. Whenever I ask what I did wrong, everyone ignores me.

I asked the therapists what I did wrong, and they told me it was because I was sick in the head, and my parents were trying to fix me. When I asked them why they had to hit me or ignore me after they had squeezed my shoulder, they told me it was because if they didn't I would never understand that I was being bad, and this is what everyone had agreed was the best thing. Everyone but me.

That is when things started to get really twisted. The therapists asked me what I hated more, the beatings or being ignored. I told them being ignored was the worst.

It was like the silence hurt my ears or something. It's hard to explain, watching others laugh and talk and not being able to be part of it.

One time, just before my mom went to hug my sibling, she came up to me on the couch and told me to watch. Afterward, she came to me and said, "I hope you see what it is like to be loved. I want to hug you and talk to you like that, but you have to be a good boy and stop walking like that. Because if you don't stop walking like that, I won't be able to talk to you ever again, and the doctors will tell me I can't love you anymore."

I watched the kids on the football team so I could start walking like them. Of course, I also took beatings for looking in their general direction.

The psychological warfare will be what sucks the life out of me over time. I know this is my fate. I just hope it doesn't drive me to the bottle or the needle or something like that.

I can't do anything about it right now, because I just have to survive each day. I guess I'll deal with all the effects of the mind games when I know I can take care of myself. For now, it's just about survival and dealing with the therapists and my parents.

Picking my own punishment was pretty common and an effective tactic to mess with my head. I'll give you an example. One time, my mom and I were shopping, and I touched a lavender dress while we were walking by the racks. As soon as we got home, she called the therapists and made me tell them what I did. The therapists told me I had to choose a punishment. They coached me through describing the dress, right down to the sensation the material gave my fingertips. Suddenly, they came to the conclusion that I should have to hold a hot teapot with my fingertips for as long as I could bear. That way, my fingertips would hurt every time I picked something up for the next couple of days.

This became a regular thing, especially in 5th and 6th grade. I think it was the doctor's way of making me think it was a good idea, or like I deserved it or something.

Sixth grade got intense, and that is when I made the mistake of telling the doctors about the beat-up camper my neighbors had stashed in the woods. The doctors gave me weird assignments. One time, they had me on the phone and told me to go and walk around the camper and see if the door was unlocked. They had me open the door and look at all the trash laying around in it. Then they asked me if I would like to live there and told me if I wanted to run away and steal the camper that no one would come after me. They sat with me on the phone for a long time, helping me play out how I would steal the camper and go live on my own on the road. They had me visualize what it would be like to run away and how I would survive, and they encouraged me every step of the way to do this.

A couple days later, when I was having a phone session with the doctors, I told them I didn't want to run away, and they were very disappointed. Before I knew it, I was analyzing baseboards again for stealing a piece of raw asparagus from the kitchen counter before my mom had cooked it.

Since I had decided I wasn't going to run away, the doctors told me I had to pick how I was going to kill myself, just in case I decided being gay was more important than my family.

By this time, I knew I had to pick and do it quick, so that I could start proving fast that I was an "All American Boy," just trying to realize "the American Dream."

I immediately chose a gun, which seemed the quickest. A few days later, not coincidentally and obviously under the instruction of the therapists, my dad showed me where the key to the gun cabinet was hidden, just in case "I ever needed to get in there to protect our family."

The therapists asked me if I wanted to off myself in the camper. I said no. I pictured myself rotting away in all that trash, and as disgusting as they think I am, I just didn't think it would do me justice.

I finally committed to the therapists that I would just

wander off on one of our weekend reservation trips and blow my brains out somewhere on a mountain ledge. They had me visualize the spot where I would do it, and what really messed with my head was when they had me close my eyes and listen to the gunshot echoing through the mountains. They had me visualize people stopping by the campfire, wondering where the gunshot came from. Then they had me visualize my parents being at home and not hearing the gunfire. Then they had me visualize which way I thought my body would fall after the bullet went through my mouth and out the back of my head.

Needless to say, these days I stick to playing nine holes instead of camping. I'll survive, I think. I'll get over having to play "manly sports" instead of joining the chess club, and someday, the bruises between my shoulder blades will be gone, and I'll hopefully be able to live the life I want, not the life they want.

The only reason I'm risking my life to write this is because I know some kids aren't strong like me. We have to protect the children, and I have to protect them. If I am apathetic about kids I know who are being abused, then I am as guilty as the abuser. I can take a lot of reality, but that I cannot accept. I would never hurt children the way they hurt me. Ever. It's not okay.

I'm asking for your help to protect these kids.

The other day I read an article, which said that something like 20% of teens attempt suicide in our state.

I wonder what the odds are that they are like me, being told by doctors and parents to kill themselves? For example, how many of them are being given the keys to the cabinet by their own father?

The law is the only thing that can stop therapists from teaching parents how to do all of this horrible stuff. My mom and dad never would have known how to torture me if the doctors hadn't told them.

Sincerely,
Between the Blades

3

A State Of Grey

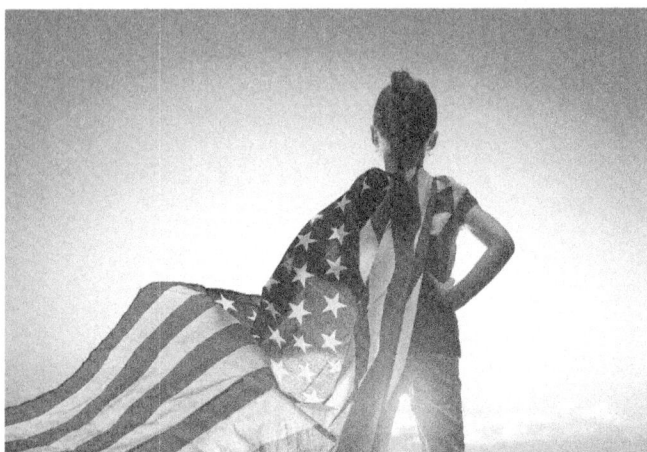

A State Of Grey

Time does not exist.
No past, nor future,
Only ever the now.
Never then, nor there,
Every moment the last.
In every last there is great love.
No fear, nor pain amidst the lasts.

There is sorrow, yes.
For it is only sorrow's line, which branches love.
No I, nor we. Only you.
My beat-less heart is beautiful.
Without the pulse of I, there is only you.
Only your every beat, heard and seen.

There is only ever you and never I.
Thy love shields your beat from the state of grey
Off you go, to the truth of time.
My beat-less heart remains behind,
Floating in the lasts.

Prisons made of stucco siding hide the drugged children who sleep
inside of them. It is in the homes where fresh mulch is laid for
flowers to die that the reflection of torture lives.

The will to die hangs on walls and the empty bookcases echo the
loneliness of the beaten. The closets of chaos are cleaned with no
release as the anchor rests in the hidden bottles of turquoise glass.
Before the mountain is the mirage.
Beautiful from a distance, the floating vision, its frequency holds
medusa's lure.
The smell of fresh cut grass leads you there,

with hammocks to rest in upon the way.
The footprints of tradition and the babies wrapped in pink and
blue plot the path to the promise of quench.
Horizontal dreams of the earth's rotation are designed to calm the
masses with illusions of fixed stars
The train arrives at the glass prison, where I am held captive by
the only childhood dreams imposed upon me.

For it was the weight of a grandparent's disappointment and the
fear of a parent's rejection and hate, which confined me to
compromise.
It was my mom's threat of "r" and her instruction of suicide,
which sent me skipping over the puddle to my own denial.
I bear the weight of my cheeks,
certain I will never know the freedom of childhood again.

I sit upon the wood, loathing the sand, which chains me.
For every grain against my feet reminds me of the youth
I was given only for the idea of who I was,
and never with intent for who I have always been.

The glass walls are meant to taunt me with a life of relief
I would never know.
I watch the walkers pass with the corners of their mouths turned
north, in blissful ignorance of the red truth.

The singer's arm is my salvation and the blood, which drips from
my fingertips, is a release. It is the red stains upon the fabric,
which tell the tale of a mother's tears and a father without a
compass.

Someday, in years to come,
the daughter will whisper the truth of the hate of children,
and as I once was, she too will bear the weight of south
upon the tide's smile.

The most truthful poetry I ever heard was the story of the boy who bore the thunder in a cave.
The most useful fear I ever faced was trying to understand where the thunder would land.
The task was to sit alone in the dark during an angry spring night and not be startled by the thunder.
To not be startled by the thunder means that you must understand what creates its violence and predict where it's angry fist will land.

The Mother of the Arts feared the summer's rise, and begged her brother to teach her daughter how to survive the echoes of the thunder in the caves.

"To not be startled by the thunder means that you must first understand what crates its violence and predict where it's angry fist will land. Do you understand?" the Weatherman asked, as the agony crawled from the throat's ridge.
"I think so," his daughter said calmly.
"How do you know?" he insisted.
"Because I know that the lullabies are not for me," the child responded with certainty.
With the sorrow's submissions, he agreed to teach the one thing he hoped he never would. How he wished she wouldn't learn the numbness of the thunder.
"I wish for it not," he said. "But we all know if you are to survive the summer of hate to come, then you must."

The storm begins, and the Weatherman first tasks his daisy to predict where the thunder will land. The girl sitting in the spring snow, eyes closed, hands grasping the ledge, just listen to the rain. Then, BOOM, the thunder punches you in the soul and shakes your body from the inside out.

The Weatherman was right. It was just like being told you were hated by the world, or hit across the face, or looked at with disgust, or having clothes ripped off your body or your body ripped off.

Sitting in the dark, waiting for the anger of the clouds to bellow, was just like knowing the fear of the sunrise.

The first storm came and went, and the shock of hate was no less. But then the second storm arrived.
I had to sit on my hands in order not to jump away.
It was then I realized my fearlessness of thunder was not enough.

The girl came running to her Mother of the Arts and the Weatherman.
   "I cannot predict where the thunder will land," she said, "and I do not think the mathematician's games can, either!"
   "You are correct, my innocent," said the Weatherman.
   "So, with that we will finish and know that the startle cannot be stopped, but only bared."

Silence took the time, and the Weatherman went to his golden room, where a picture of Les Miserables was sketched for him in lead.
   "Mother," Willow whispered. "Please do not tell the Weatherman, but I am no longer startled by the thunder."
   "I know, my child," the Mother of the Arts sighed with relief. "How did you do it?"
   "I opened my hands, grasping nothing, as I waited for the thunder's closeness. With the freedom of my palms, I traced the thunder's startle through my veins to my core, and then, I let the violence of the clouds inside my soul.

Suddenly, I could bear the rage of the thunder. You see, the only way to not be startled by the hate is to turn the thunder from a punch into a blade. It was when I allowed my soul to bleed that I

knew I could bear the weight of whatever conversion would come.
For it is the blood from my soul which silences the thunder."

With the numbness of thunder comes the silence I had never
known.
How strange to know the relief of fading sounds.
When shielded by true deafness, comes the friendship of smell
and the beloved curse of foresight.

American Psychiatric Association Defines Child Psychological Abuse

In 2013, the American Psychological Association (APA) added Child Psychological Abuse to the *DSM-5 Guidebook: The Essential Companion to the Diagnostic and Statistical Manual of Mental Disorders*, describing it as "non-accidental verbal or symbolic acts by a child's parent or caregiver that result, or have reasonable potential to result, in significant psychological harm to the child."

This came nearly 20 years after The American Professional Society on the Abuse of Children defined child psychological abuse as "terrorizing, isolating, corrupting, denying emotional responsiveness, or "a repeated pattern of extreme incidents that convey to children that they are worthless, flawed, unloved, unwanted, or only of value in meeting another's needs."

Experts have defined the cumulative effects of this abuse as the production of psychological and social defects in the growth of a child.

Sources: Donald W. Black and Jon E. Grant, *DSM-5 Guidebook: The Essential Companion to the Diagnostic and Statistical Manual of Mental Disorders*, 5th ed. (Arlington, VA: American Psychiatric Publishing, 2014), 423; John E. B. Myers, *The APSAC Handbook on Child Maltreatment*, 3d ed. (Los Angeles: Sage, 2011), 126–30.

FROM: Child victim Of conversion therapy
TO: Indiana State Legislature, U.S. Congress

July 13, 2018

Dear Elected Officials,

I am almost 18 and I love my high school, and I am loved. The teachers are impressive and bring us all together. What is really cool about it is how they let the students lead the way. Whoever came up with their master plan is pretty smart, and it's totally working, and I am so lucky.

But here is the deal: I am just a short time away from going to the voting booths and pulling the lever of the future to put it in your hands, and I am afraid it will mean nothing. In my head, I hear the great leaders of this world echo great lines like these:

"The work of today is the history of tomorrow, and we are its makers," Juliette Gordon Low;

"It is a queer thing, but imaginary troubles are harder to bear than actual ones," Dorothea Dix;

"The glory of each generation is to make its own precedents," Bleva Ann Lockwood;

"I shall never do a man's work for less than a man's pay," Clara Barton;

"The cause of freedom is not the cause of a race or a secret, a party or a class. It is the cause of human kind; the very birthright of humanity," Anna Julia Cooper;

"Optimism is the faith that leads to achievement," Helen Keller;

"The most difficult thing is the decision to act; the rest is merely tenacity," Amelia Earhart;

"The most courageous act is still to think for yourself aloud," Coco Chanel;

"It is much easier to apologize than it is to get permission," Grace Hopper;

"If I have accomplished anything in life it is because I have been willing to work hard," Madame C.J. Walker.

"As long as you keep a person down, some part of you has to be down there to hold him down, so it means you cannot soar as you otherwise might," Marian Anderson;

"Women who stepped up were measured as citizens of the nation, not as women…This was a people's war, and everyone was in it," Oveta Culp Hobby;

"People sometimes feel insignificant and doubt they can make a difference in the world. Well, believe me, one person can," Mary Kay Ash;

"If society will not admit of woman's free development, then society must be remodeled," Dr. Elizabeth Blackwell;

"I never doubted that equal rights were the right direction. Most reforms, most problems are complicated. But to me there is nothing complicated about ordinary equality," Alice Paul;

"The greater part of our happiness or misery depends on our dispositions and not our circumstances," Martha Washington;

"Life shrinks or expands in proportion to one's courage," Anais Nin;

"It is never too late to be what you might have been," Mary Anne Evans;

"We can change the world with words," Maya Angelou.

But what is the point of voting if people come and speak in your Houses and tell you, "I have been abused as a child, and I need protection," and you do nothing to protect them?

Leaders of Indiana, I am confused as to why Indiana

has not passed the conversion therapy protection laws, which have been brought before you. Why not?

I am not gay. In fact, I am in a heterosexual relationship and do not struggle with the battles I watch sum people fight every day. But I do not want to lose my friend. I do not want him to kill himself, and your laws are making it okay for his family to force him to do that.

Representatives of Indiana, I write you this letter, hoping it will mean something. If the laws change and protect the kids in your schools, then I know my vote will matter, and you will have it. But if the laws do not change, then I will know this letter means nothing to you, and neither does my vote.

Make no mistake: The youth in America is a united group, and it is at the polls that you will either have our unified voice of support or protest. None of us want our friends to be hurt anymore, and we are telling you this, AGAIN. Whether you have our vote at the polls in November or not, will be up to you.

Please remember: YOUR VOTE COUNTS TO US.

Sincerely,
Almost 18 Years Old

4
The Ugly

The Ugly

To know the agony of choosing a writing instrument is to know
the ugliness which lingers in the unset sunset.
The only thing more painful than the orange mountain, is the
moment you know the weight of lead, nestled in your blood.
To know the smell inside the homes of Mirado, is to know true
weakness.

I have always known the hate.
Its blunt objects have riddled my legs with bruises for as long as I
have known the sunset.
The demon's vomit upon the reed has elicited the song of loneliness
since I built my home in the corner of darkness upon thy princess
bed.

The smell of burnt zucchini laid the tracks upon my back since
victory was mine.
The wire chains clenched my jaw just before the proposal of child
pawn or poverty beat me.

I have known the hate since the devil's call for my innocence.
You see, the putrid smog weaves around the flowerless children
who do not know the love of seed, in hopes that puncturing their
innocence will suffocate their lungs.

I have known the murderer's trigger pull since the sleeping
whispers willed my suicide.
The desert storm of my life is a covert battle, whose front is filled
with smiles and gift-wrapped tokens of farce love.

My battle is fought in a still wind and beneath a cool, bright sun.
The battle of conversion is the curse of Christmas trees decorated
with homemade ornaments and plump stockings, hidden behind
the couch, stuffed with tears and terror.

Consider tomorrow today and the future will be grey.
Consider not and the black and white's weight will stay.

The Bull's Eye seeks its karmic right to charge the arrow to
deflect the iron's momentum.
The facade of right to privacy is the mask you mold to hide the
secrets you ask your victims to keep.
It is only when we catch on the flip side that life after hide begins…
and the notes dance upon the sandpaper's course.

It is the weaver of the rocking chairs that are the ones who teach
their children to hear the heartbeat of mind over matter.

The Master of the Crayon factory lined the playing field in hopes
the arena would shield the team from the hailstorm of their lives.

The team of daughters, coached by the parade of parents, pounced
upon the mountain and the puzzles pieces of purpose are laid out,
as the mission realizes that board games are not for child's play.

The Bridge stands to bind and facilitate the pieces to find their
way to their fitted fate, as the carousel of madness continues.

The scapegoat is simply the one who has enough arm strength to
endure holding the mirror to the back of the onlooker.
It is sad, what it will take for you to see the reflection, for it will
take you knowing the anguish of a child's death to see the
unconditional love of the sons and daughters, which you discard.

Dear Child,

The hate before you is unavoidable.
You must walk into the flames, as it is your fate.

I say I love you.

Because I love you, I will light the fire for you to burn in.

Because I love you, I will let the skin melt from your bones.

Because I love you, I will give the mob the bats to beat you with.

Because I love you, I will terrorize you.

Because I love you, I will shackle you with threads of deception.

Because I love you, I will bind your jaw with my iron fist.

Because I love you, I will never praise you.

Because I love you, I will loathe you.

Because I love you, I will keep you ignorant from the world.

Because I love you, I will impose extremism on your innocence.

Because I love you, I will commence your violation.

Because I love you, I will always know you are not innocent.

Because I love you, I will demonize you.

Because I love you, I will teach you the spot to press the gun against your temple.

Because I love you, I will abandon you not once, not twice, but thrice.

Because I love you, I will distort the mirror before you.

Because I love you, I will ignore you, rather than disown you.

Because I love you, I will humiliate the people you like.

Because I love you, I will hate you.

And you will live happily ever after, honey.

Love, mom

Isolation

Isolation is often used to facilitate power and control over someone for an abusive purpose. Isolation reduces the opportunity of the abused to be rescued or escape from the abuse. It also helps disorientate the abused and makes the abused more dependent on the abuser.

An important element of psychological control is the isolation of the victim from the outside world. Isolation includes controlling a person's social activity: who they see, who they talk to, where they go and any other method to limit their access to others. It may also include limiting what material is read. It can include insisting on knowing where they are and requiring permission for medical care. The abuser exhibits hypersensitive and reactive jealously.

Sources: Claudia Garcia-Moreno et al., *Global and Regional Estimates of Violence Against Women: Prevalence and Health Effects of Intimate Partner Violence and Non-partner Sexual Violence* (Geneva: World Health Organization, 2013), 7; Ben Atherton-Zeman, "Power and Control Wheel for Men Working to End Gender Based Violence," based on the Duluth Model and to be used in conjunction with it, n.d., http://www.ncdsv.org/images/VM_Power-and-control-wheel-for-men-working-to-end-GBV-male-accountability-wheel.pdf.

FROM: Child victim Of conversion therapy
TO: Colorado State Legislature, U.S. Congress

December 31, 2017

Dear Elected Officials,

I really try my hardest to fit in. It goes one of three ways in a big school district: Either you deal with the pressure of standing out, you deal with the pressure of blending in, or, you deal with the pressure of being discovered. I'm the latter.

My high school tried really hard. The teachers care, and I've seen them do amazing things for students. Sometimes I would look at them and wonder what it must feel like to have their hands tied and not be able to help the students they know need help. I mean, there are so many of us, but I know they would do more if they could, legally, you know. But they can't break the boundaries for one kid, as that would leave too many behind.

I'm here to tell a quick story about an attempt to create a boy crazy teenager.

This is the deal with conversion techniques. The people who do it are stealth, and sometimes you don't even know what's going down.

One day, my dad was at the therapist with me before my soccer game. The therapist said we were going to try something, and it involved my dad not hugging me and not talking to me for a while. The therapists said my dad had to do this in order to make me behave like a good teenager. He explained it would take time, so my dad would be acting like this for a while. As it turned out, not only my dad, but

also my mom and siblings, were assigned to
They all did a good job, and the ho'
Whenever I walked into a room, everyo_
Were you ever in a room and people just kept acu..ₒ
you weren't there? Literally, no one even makes eye contact
with you, and they just keep going about their conversation
and make no effort to include you. It's weird. Like you are
sitting on the stage in the middle of a play but you are not
a character, and everyone just keeps acting the scenes out
in front of you like you are a silent prop.

My family pretty much didn't talk to me at all in
elementary school or junior high. What's really disturbing
is the efforts my parents went to in order to keep me
isolated from the community. And to keep other children
from talking to me. It was extreme. I wasn't allowed to
socialize with other kids, except the ones who knew what
to say and what not to say. I had no social contact with my
peers until I joined organized school sports.

When I asked my dad why he didn't talk to me, he
just ignored me. The therapists had designated my mom
as the person I was allowed to ask questions.

This is part of their play and manipulation. They
allow a child to pick one person to ask questions and get
instructions from, and we are not allowed to talk to
anyone else, and if I ever tried I would be punished.

In the beginning, I tried to talk to my family, but my
mom's response of yelling at me became too much, and
it just wasn't worth the effort anymore.

I eventually just stopped asking why people didn't
talk to me or why my dad didn't love me, because I knew
I would just get yelled at or sent away.

I hated being sent to my room. I knew I would have
to stay there for hours and hours, sometimes days, and it
got way too lonely. I started to ask my mom the same

questions I would ask my teachers, in an effort to have some kind of conversation.

I thought if I asked good questions she would talk to me. That didn't work, either. Her response to everything eventually became, "go look it up." She got really good at dismissing me so that she didn't have to talk to me at all.

She told me that my asking questions was going to get her in trouble and make it seem like she wasn't doing a good job at what the therapists told her to do. My parents were supposed to keep track of the times I spoke and when they spoke to me. That way, the doctors could evaluate if they were "achieving effective isolation or not."

I remember hearing my mom talking to the therapists on the phone and saying those words. Suddenly, it all became real in that moment. I stopped asking any questions at all and found out other ways to learn what I wanted to learn. Before I knew it, I didn't have a reason to talk and had accepted that I wasn't "Daddy's little girl."

The efforts didn't achieve what they intended. I never became boy crazy, but they sure tried. Between withholding affection, shoving "Dear Diary" boyfriend love stories down my throat and keeping me isolated from almost everyone in the world, they stayed very busy making a constant effort to change me.

Their efforts were not without fail, though. No doubt part of their intention was to make me feel unwanted. It worked, because I definitely do.

I spend much of my day battling rejection now. With every person I come into contact with, my first thought is why don't they like me, or are they going to say something mean to me because I'm disgusting or an idiot?

It's almost a little shocking now when people talk to me like a regular person. I'm just not used to it. I try and dodge the "interaction bullets" as much as I can, for fear I will get struck by one. Shoot, I just realized that this is probably just what the therapist wants.

This really is a long story, and I'm gonna bounce right now and go to the shopping center and hope not to get caught.

I hope this letter helps someone understand what really happens in conversion therapy, and that it helps make it illegal for therapists to teach families to do this kind of thing.

Every little girl deserves to be a princess.

Sincerely,
No One's Little Girl

5

The Beauty of May

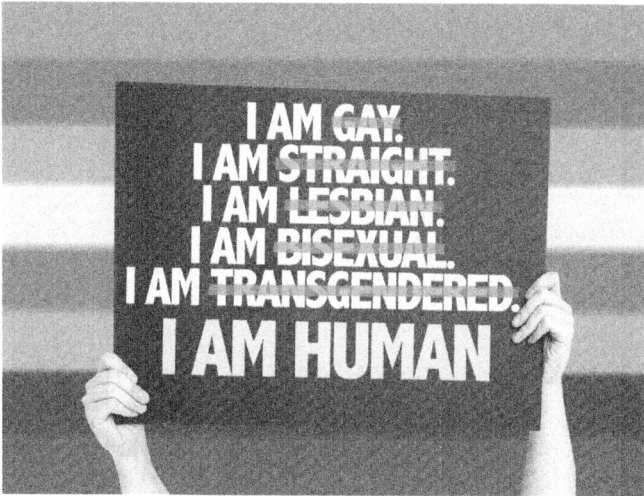

The Beauty Of May

*It was during first grade when the artistry of May first struck me,
and poetry was born.*
That is the thing about poetry—it only lives between two people.
Poetry is only ever you and I.

*As true as the shark's deliberation, are the symbiotic lines of our
poetry, that will only ever be known between you and I.*

*With the knowledge of the earth beneath me as a child,
walking bare foot for the first time, comes the sting of
the dead grass and the whispers of the women of the
world, that I have always ever heard.*

*It is the women of the world who give sound to the white space,
frost to the lost and the skipping tiptoes within a few breaths of
the table that is as lovely as honey dripping off a fork in the
summer sun.*

*It is the women of the world who remind me of the conversations
between the words from times past, that I so longed for.*

It is the women of the world who whisper to me from the sun.
*It is the women of the world who show me the shades of blue and
green, red and brown, and the building's shade of light.*

How beautiful to feel the instinct to care for her.
How inspiring to only know of the color of her hair in the sun.
*How precious to know the difference in her cheeks, the exposure of
her teeth, the curve of her bridge and then in the softness of the
colors setting on the curved corners of a woman through the
classroom glass.*

How titillating to be driven to insanity by her smell.

48

How lovely to be flattered by her presence…
How lovely to flatter her presence.
How lovely to close my eyes and always see her eyes.
How lovely to draw an oval under her instruction.

She was the first role of lighting I had heard since I saw a blade of grass. It was the 13th summer and suddenly the world was illuminated by her lighting's strike. The seasons danced around her, and children frolicked at her fingertips as she sent the air of harvest to us all.

I had been read to by a lovely stranger on the streets in a time past, but never before by a scholar.

And then, the sound of study came into my life.

The music played from the pages and I became an instrumentalist for the first time. I began to beat my drum, from snare to cymbal, back to base—right foot, left foot, stage up, bar one, back to gut wrenching bass, look down, look up—and take your kneeled seat.

I would later run to her for protection from the son's inability to respond with emotional appropriateness, which would demand my freedom.

It would be the teachings of The Field and echoes of .L, who sent me running to my survival. Just before I did, she looked at me and knew, that now, I knew that vampires exist.

Once I was her child, and with the teachings of the Geologist, I learned the truth of the texture of stone against my blood.

Now I knew the illusion of velvet and the face of terror in her lungs.

The fun of fickle is not child's play at all.
For it is the fickle which is the father of violation.

It is this knowledge that every mother hopes to never share with her daughter's stare.
It is the women of the world who the daughters read the unwritten words of fairy tales.
It was in the sadness of gold I saw a mother's sunrise break a women's heart.
It was in the chill of her luminosity that I realized the sadness of soaring love.
And it was when she opened up her jewelry box that she knew her daughter would never hear her mother's goodbye.

It was in the weight of round that I saw my truth again.
It was in her circled steps I saw panic surface as the familiarity of the unknown haunted her from windows past.
It was in her eight steps that she swaddled the love of the game, as she remained the essence of loving.
It was the winter eclipse that froze the foot of powdered snow for her to stand upon.
It was the spring moon, which whispered it was time to travel the sidewalk.
It was the lullaby of the forest, which cleared the way for the young.

But it is first, her voice, which taught me of unconditional love.

WHO Declares Emergency

According to the *2015 Prevention Resource Guide: Making Meaningful Connections*, the World Health Organization (WHO) defines child abuse and child maltreatment as "All forms of physical and/or emotional ill-treatment, sexual abuse, neglect or negligent treatment or commercial or other exploitation, resulting in actual or potential harm to the child's health, survival, development, or dignity in the context of a relationship of responsibility, trust or power."

The WHO defines physical abuse as "intentional use of physical force against a child that results in or has a high likelihood of resulting in harm to the child's health, survival, development, or dignity. This includes hitting, beating, kicking, shaking, biting, strangling, scalding, burning, poisoning, and suffocating. Much physical violence against children in the home is inflicted with the object of punishing."

Sources: Claudia Garcia-Moreno et al., *Global and Regional Estimates of Violence Against Women: Prevalence and Health Effects of Intimate Partner Violence and Non-partner Sexual Violence* (Geneva: World Health Organization, 2013), 7; Ben Atherton-Zeman, "Power and Control Wheel for Men Working to End Gender Based Violence," based on the Duluth Model and to be used in conjunction with it, n.d., http://www.ncdsv.org/images/VM_Power-and-control-wheel-for-men-working-to-end-GBV-male-accountability-wheel.pdf.

FROM: Child victim Of conversion therapy
TO: Office of the Governor, Kansas State Legislature,
U.S. Congress

November 8, 2017

Dear Governor,

I write this letter to you, and not to all those other people
in the House. I hope you know how hard this letter is for
me to write. I am glad you cannot see my tears. I am
afraid writing this letter will hurt you, too, because the
things that make it up are so hurtful that even if you don't
experience it, it still hurts you. I am sorry if this letter
hurts you.

The therapists make me take really cold baths. When
I asked why my brothers don't have to take the baths,
they said because girls need ice cold baths because we are
more likely to be sick than boys. The cold hurts bad. But
if I don't sit in the baths for as long as they tell me, they
will hit my legs when I get out.

Have you ever had anyone hit your legs after they
have been soaking in ice-cold water? It hurts so bad, not
just my legs, but all over my body. It even hurts my jaw,
when they hit my legs after I get out of the bath.

The therapists say that they have to check my pants,
after they make me watch the videos. That's what started
the baths. But now I am really sad because I have to take
the showers, before they make me lie down.

I don't want to lie down anymore for my uncle, or
any of the boys. But my mom checked my pants one day
after I was playing with my friend, who I had described
to my mom as pretty, and she said the doctors told her I
had to lie down now, in order for me to prove my body
responds to boys.

Governor, I don't want to lie down anymore.

I don't want to go to the therapists anymore.

Can you at least tell my parents that I will take the baths and they can hit me on the legs, but that I don't have to lie down anymore?

Sincerely,
The Girl in the Crowd

6

Thirteen Steps

Thirteen Steps

I had never stood nor sat before, only fluttered my wings.
I was not the words, merely the fairy, resting upon them.
It was once the blades of grass, which smelled of chocolate, that
cushioned my feet before the poetry took shade.

"Look down," the whisper came from the grey space.

Chin to chest, I saw the soil and rock for the first time.
The weighted world was their gift to me, meant to protect me from
the force of the future by slowly grading away the innocents of my feet.

The rain no longer fell upon me from the heavens.
The rain no longer danced in the clouds.
The view was no longer a gaze, forever the view was now a
command.
The rain now rises from the soil to move the stones, and rest
amongst the fortunes told.

It was the panic of the earth's layers, which jolted me into the ground.
The air was gone and now there was fire and ash.
Steppingstones to the seat of flight bear fear to nestle my bottom.
Now it is the sound of sail, which consumes my sense.

Crouched at the base of closed doors, children learn the pain of
love from their parents.

Eight steps up, I found my desire to know.
On the seventh step, I saw how awesome the sum really is.
Sitting on step number six, I felt the anger within me for the first time.

On the fifth step, I saw where I was for the first time in my life—
behind me, where I had come from. Beneath me, the treacherous
steppingstones were laid out along the journey back to life. Before
me, laid the truth of the frost.

On the fourth step, I saw my reflection in the mirror before me for the first time, and I realized I would someday write the poetry of walking on the blood-soaked battlefields.

It was on the third step that I met my ambition to soar.

On the second step, I weaved a toolbox to harbor knowledge, the only weapon I would ever need.

On the first step, I learned that calm is the only tool with the power to control fear.

At the base of the steps, I saw there was no end to the journey and I embraced the virtue of patience.

It is on the edge of every step I take, which I commit to the courage in my reflection.

On the ninth step, I realized how fortunate I was to sit at a dinner table set to dine.

On step ten, I was passed the gift of hope and played upon the silver-lined playing fields, encircled in five interlocking rings that give all children a chance to covet dreams.

On the eleventh step, I sat the longest, trying to find a way to bear the sadness, which consumes me at the sight of people sitting at a table with no settings.

On step twelve, I saw the corruption of our forests, as I realized Pandora's box was made of whittled wood and sits as the centerpiece of most dining room tables.

It is the thirteenth step I cherish most.
For it was on this step, I first felt my smile…
and the beauty within me.

Neglect

Child neglect is the failure of a parent or other person with responsibility for the child, to provide needed food, clothing, shelter, medical care, or supervision, to the degree that the child's health, safety or well-being may be threatened with harm. Neglect is also lack of attention from the people surrounding a child, and the non-provision of the relevant and adequate necessities for the child's survival, which would be a lacking in attention, love and nurture.

Source: D. Theoklitou, N. Kabitsis, and A, Kabitsi, "Physical and Emotional Abuse of Primary School Children by Teachers," *Child Abuse & Neglect* 36, no. 1 (2012): 64–70.

FROM: Child victim Of conversion therapy
TO: Missouri State Legislature, U.S. Congress

January 3, 2018

Dear Elected Officials,

Have you ever really thought about the components of a question? I spent a considerable amount of time doing this as a child. You see, questions are the force of the key's turn, and perhaps what Einstein sought to formulate with $E=Mc2$.

People often believe that it is the door you stand before or the road that you take, which bears the heavy weight of fate.

But this is not the case. It is the question-makers who are the key designers, the questions which dictate our direction, and the answers, which determine what will be. Perhaps you already know this, because after all, we all have answered to Robert Frost.

And then, there is a question's muse.

What magnificence and torture the many must have seen, to create such questions which have birthed the world today.

It is often said that the muse is unknown to the self, but is known by many.

My mom is a key of questioning wonder. The child's question she birthed was: "What does it feel like to be hugged?" You see, hugging is what I chose to give up so that I could stay and live with my parents and not have to go to a foster home.

The doctors said that if I wasn't going to run away, I had to pick a punishment that would be equal to the pain I was causing my parents, because according to them, someday when I grew up I was going to choose to be a lesbian instead of loving my family.

I couldn't understand why I was being punished for something I hadn't done yet, but I wasn't about to argue.

I saw a show on *Animal Planet* that said if monkeys didn't receive "hugs" they could die.

Needless to say, the therapists were pleased with my choice in punishment.

There was also the time when my mom, who appears perfectly normal to someone looking in from the outside, made me pack a bag and hit the woods. She said she couldn't stand me.

The therapists suggested I try living in the woods so that I could find out that I would be okay if I ran away. It's funny the things you pack after you have accepted that history will repeat itself, and you have now become a displaced person.

I don't know why I thought my music box would be important in the wild, but I guess those are the priorities of little kids.

Anyway, I never did run away. Now, I just live with the fear of being sent away.

After all, this is a much more PC solution for a family of my stature. But it won't go on forever. I'll be out of here in no time, or will I?

These are the life lessons that taught me about the sun dial and what mine is composed of: cobblestone, sweat, cold, heartbeat, wet grass, dry bark, time, terror, angry, hungry, sad, cobblestone, mud, morning, so sad, death (?), no time, darkness, frogs and snakes, shivering, circles, hopeless submission, silence.

The most disturbing part about all of this is that my mom actually works with kids. If the therapists can convince her that it's a good idea to abuse me—her own child—then what makes you think that the children she gets paid to deal with aren't in danger, too? After all, she is being trained to be an abuser of children by mental health professionals who are surely perverting mental health techniques.

All I can say is, I hope, for your own children's sake, that your kids aren't under her care.

Sincerely,
Frozen in Time

7

Darkness & Lights?

Darkness & Lights?

"Close your eyes, wish with all your might, and if you're lucky,
when you wake, you will know the life I always wanted.
If you are smart, you will create a world without you in it for
yourself," the Octopus hisses, as disdain seeps from her tentacles to
capture the voice and imprison the voiceless.

With the summer solstice came the first silent stent of the
puppeteer.
The Matriarch orchestrates the scene and sets the stage, once more,
for the conversion of hate to proceed.

Seated beside the family's branch, the innocent are required to
prove the direction of their course has no turns and the intent to
travel is within the bounds of social norm.
The oath to travel down the straight and narrow is taken with the
hand's force and with the fear of a sister's death in heart.

What sacrifice will come is unfathomable to most, but this is the
bread which the colorful children are offered.
While most young enjoy the many grains of culture, the abandoned
must choose between mold or starvation.
It was with the hope for the sister to become a ballerina that I
chose to stay and turn my innocence over to the devil.

Mother Nature rages today, using the bay to warn the inconsiderate.
Her current of disappointment has no mercy as it tears through
the lowlands and dominates the man-made intrusion of concrete
and machinery. She does not speak with a soft breeze today, for
her warnings come with each mighty gust of wind.

Be wary of the wind and water today, for the Mother weeps from
the apathy and erupts from the intolerant.
Be wary of the wind and water today, for it is only the Watchman
who is safe traveling the streets when the Mother rages.

The nighttime Service Lights position themselves behind the curtain.

Out of the sky appears the Black Bird from the fire's scorn and perches itself on her gated heart, as it pounds the notes of Whiplash.

The Black Bird remains guarding his post, and in turn is comforted by the grace of a gentle sway.

The World around is deaf to their spoken glance and their silent exchange is a comfort only to one another. Best for the company they keep that deafness remains.

For some things, the world is better off not knowing, and only shared among the glance of those who know the merciless.

Be fooled not by the silent crow, for it is the vengeance of the Wild Glide.

As the clock strikes four, the flames echo long and far and proclaim: "Fair thee warning to all, for it is the root of J and the roar of the t-gun, which protect the heart of our Willow."

It is you, the vicious, who send Mother earth to rage, and I who come to warn the inconsiderate, affront the gusts of wind, and guide the flood waters around the willow's trunk to shield the fragile branches from the tears, which swell the bay.

Fair thee warning to the inconsiderate, the winds wrath knows no temper when the branches of the Willow are tampered with.

Fair thee warning to the inconsiderate, "I am the Glide of the wind and the Willow belongs to the Fleet of Three."

Without the weep of darkness, the flowers would not bloom.
The Keeper of the Colors starts the stroke of the fairytale as the

65

thirteenth hour begins its countdown.
The mouse jumps from the corn stalks clock set at Eleven, to
waken the Zoo's patrons to a world that does not yet exist, with
the knowledge of the hateful love.
Perched by a window, the naive realizes she is looking at a set,
and a set was all it ever was.

Crouched in the corner is the reverberation of a mom's instructions
to jump off a bridge.

"Do I breathe or weep through that moment?"
the traveler asks herself.

"Would I jump or would I hope in everything but her hateful
love?"

It is the hate of mothers,
which teach the children about the cruelty of war.

The tainted fingertips live on Vietnam street, just past the picket
fences on Everest's court.

"Mind over Matter," The Master of the Wood Floors teaches, in
the hope of arming the ones who miss the feeling of something they
have never known.
How strange, to know vulnerability at both the hands of the
harsh and the harsh-less.
They say the bad outweighs the good, but in the trenches, the good
does in fact outweigh the evil.
For it is the heartbeat of the ones who lead with empathy, which
foster the survival of the wounded.

It is the advisers of yesterday and the educators of tomorrow who
wrap today in their silence, hoping the shield they provide will be
enough for the locust to write of another season.

The beds are made of roses that rest in the nest atop the Director's Dedication.

The Wizard whispers to the girl and makes the Master of Magnificence known to the world. The Wizard is cloaked with the power of fate. Her spells are a force amongst the masses, and not to be doubted. Her soft whisper gently rocks the willow's branches back and forth, like a newborn in her cradle.

It has always been the whisper of the woods and the cornfields, that brought life to the branches of the willow tree.

How strange, to wake up from a trance of survival, when suddenly the white noise is so loud and clear.
How I long for a world without clarity of sound and sight again.

There is safety in the shadows, but no light to grow from.
"Happy Birthday" they sing, but they should say, "It is your birthday," for the song of birth in threes is too sad for ears to hear.

As I see the face of love in the night sky, I know I am the change I wished to see in the world.
That is the beauty of my birth, for even from the ash, I fought for the freedom of those who are chained in social prisons.

I feel my heart fully again, and no part of me remains sleeping. The memories flood my mind like a raging river, swollen from a child's anguish. The pain is too great to sleep any longer.

How fortunate to know the love of Sum and Butterflies.
How devastating to know the truth of time and takers.
I am humbled by the greatness of connectivity and shattered by the impulses of hate.

Corporal Punishment

Corporal punishment involves hitting (smacking, slapping, spanking) children, with the hand or with an implement- whip, stick, belt, shoe, wooden spoon, etc. But it can also involve, for example, kicking, shaking or throwing children, scratching, pinching, biting, pulling hair or boxing ears, forcing children to stay in uncomfortable positions, burning, scalding, or forced ingestion.

Source: Helen Noh Anh,"Cultural Diversity and the Definition of Child Abuse," 28, in R. P. Barth, Jill Duerr Berrick, and Neil Gilbert, eds., *Child Welfare Research Review* (New York: Columbia University Press, 1994).

FROM: Child victim Of conversion therapy
TO: State of Massachusetts General Assembly, U.S. Congress

March 19, 2018

Dear Elected Officials,

First, thanks for hearing me out. A lot of kids feel this way. It's like some youth are trapped between the old and the new. Most want to hang out with each other, but our parents would kill us if we did. Like if my mom knew it wouldn't of bothered me to play on the same team with the kids not like me, she would probably have disown me for that, too. It's crazy how good everyone here is at not looking at someone they don't know or shouldn't know. It's like we are all trained to avoid eye contact. If nothing else comes out of this, all I have to say is everyone needs to start looking everyone else in the eyes and stop looking away from each other.

No matter who you are, where you are from, or who is in front of you, just look them in the eye. You can see all you need to know about a person by looking into their eyes and not looking away.

I'm sure a lot of you have seen the "you've gone and pissed me off now" face, and what comes after it from your parents. Most of you Congress people probably know what it is like to get hit in the face, too. You know that moment when you are in a car accident and everything slows down and you hear the metal crunch. You know it's bad when life goes into slow motion. I guess that's how I would describe getting hit in the face. It's the torture of slow motion and crunching metal.

Discipline, redirection, or corporal punishment?

I suppose this is why you are all debating if laws

should interfere with "parenting techniques," if that's what you want to call it.

Here's the truth: At the start of the day, I inhaled the smell of being a rich kid on the way to school, and at the end of the day, my parents were equipped with instructions from my therapists about when to hit me, what they should use to hit me with, where it should happen, and most importantly, why they should do it.

When: Regardless of the time of the offense, the punishment of choice will occur just before bedtime.

Where: Always in my bedroom, behind closed doors, by the window, which is covered by trees.

What & Why: Face-hitting would be used when I was rebellious about doing any conversion homework assignments or following any of the conversion rules. Spanking occurred whenever I tried to wear something they considered gross. Belt-spanking when I did something out in public, like sit too close to a boy. Kicking my legs whenever I looked at another kid for too long.

I tried not to make them really angry. That's when the slow motion would last for days and all rules were out the door, and I was lucky if I didn't follow.

I'll never forget the time when I told the doctors I thought the boy was beautiful. That's when I learned to take a punch in the gut like a man.

"I'm going to punch you in the gut for every single time you have thought that a boy was beautiful. So son, how many?"

I picked 11, 'because I was eleven. He gave me 12.

Sincerely,
One to Grow On

More Than 57,000 LGBT Youth Will Undergo Gay Conversion Therapy Before They Turn 18

Samantha Manzella 1/25/2018

A study released in January 2018 is providing disturbing insight into just how many young Americans are subjected to conversion therapy, the widely debunked effort to change sexual orientation or gender identity. According to the Williams Institute at UCLA, before they turn eighteen, 57,000 teens will likely undergo conversion therapy from clergy, religious counselors, or other unlicensed people. Some 20,000 will actually undergo the treatment from licensed health care professionals. (Nearly 700,000 adults have already been subjected to conversion therapy; 350,000 of them were teens at the time.)

Sources: Christy Mallory, Taylor N.T. Brown and Kerith J. Conron, "Conversion Therapy and LGBT Youth," executive summary, Williams Institute, UCLA School of Law, January 2018, https://williamsinstitute.law.ucla.edu/wp-content/uploads/Conversion-Therapy-LGBT-Youth-Jan-2018.pdf; Curtis M. Wong, "Nearly 700,000 Americans Have Been Subjected to Conversion Therapy, Report Finds," *Huffington Post*, January 29, 2018, https://www.huffingtonpost.com/entry/conversion-therapy-lgbtq-youth-study_us_5a6f549ee4b0ddb658c929.

FOR: The L.G.B.T.Q. Community
FROM: Vellah Jones
TO: America's Caretakers

February 28, 2018

Dear Caretakers,

We were offended then by your conditional love,
and we are offended still.

Do you see the reflection before you?

Thank you for your time,
VELLAH JONES

8

What If?

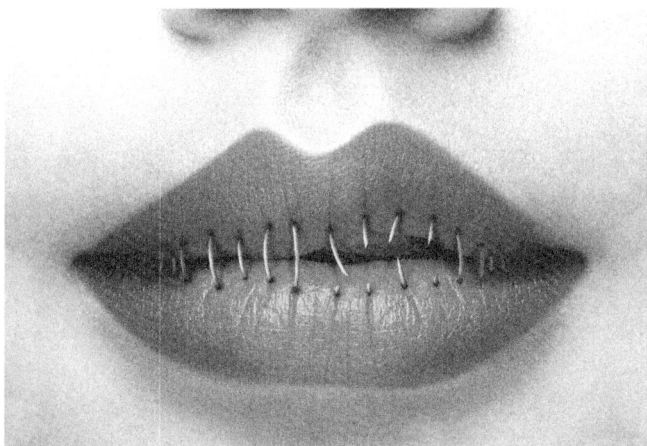

What If?

What if you lived inside a mural?
What if your blood was made of paint?
What if the water was made of sulfites?
What if the truth was so brutal the arts had no choice but to
paint you a fairytale so that your heart wouldn't shatter?
What if the world was in your grasp but the burn scars on your
fingertips left you without touch?
What if the world was so beautiful but you felt the darkness in
your reflection and saw the shadow in your steps?

The images of sadness are many in this world.
But the saddest that I know is the princess who fields the red
roses, which make our necks jolt.
For it is only the thorn's puncture, which can cause a pillow to
bleed.
Makes you wonder of the man of men who lust for red.

The weight of the broken porcelain dolls is heavy in the child's
backpack, as she glides across the moon dust.
The drought depletes the glass prison, and the open air is like
drowning in a shallow tub, relentless is the horror of the red
dessert.

The costumes of the soldiers of hate are a force to be reckoned
with. Their organized community cloaks itself in threads of
kindness, fooling even the most genuine foot traveler.

But their masks of love, which mask the hate, are their greatest
weapons.
The makers of the masks are the ones who write the evil of lawless
morals.
Their power to deceive orchestrates the murder of children by way

of taxonomic ranks and implemented suicide.
It is the makers of the masks of love who steal laughter from
children.

I remember when my heart first broke.
It was when I saw the hate in love for the first time.
It was when she looked down at me and I realized it was a mask
of love she wore as a weapon to hate me with.

To see the hate in love is to see a mother's face become a cyclone in
the desert's fangs.
The horror is unspeakable…the consequences…a child only
knowing life with a broken heart.

The only thing more terrifying then seeing the terror in someone's
lungs is seeing a child whose laughter has been lost.
When you don't feel the connection of your own umbilical cord,
it's hard to imagine creating one of your own.
The needles stung and it took one to know one.
I hope no one ever knows the horror of the truth that lies in the
discomfort of the bread against one's fingertips…

Sexual Abuse of Children on the Rise

Child sexual abuse (CSA) is a form of child abuse in which an adult or older adolescent abuses a child for sexual stimulation. Forms of CSA include asking or pressuring a child to engage in sexual activities (regardless of the outcome), indecent exposure of the genitals to a child, displaying pornography to a child, actual sexual contact with a child, physical contact with the child's genitals, viewing of the child's genitalia without physical contact, or using a child to produce child pornography.

Sources: J. Martin et al., "Asking About Child Sexual Abuse: Methodological Implications of a Two Stage Survey," *Child Abuse & Neglect* 17, no. 3 (1993): 383–92. doi:10.1016/0145-2134(93)90061-9.

FROM: Child victim Of conversion therapy
TO: Florida State Legislature, U.S. Congress

April 16, 2018

Dear Elected Officials,

I have to begin this letter by saying that this will be one of the hardest things I will ever do.

You know the techniques that advertisers use with commercials and billboards to make people think they want to buy their product by exposing it to them again and again? This was the idea behind my "sexual desires therapy sessions," as my mom called it. The therapists told me and my parents that I needed to be exposed to heterosexual behavior in order to train my brain into desiring the opposite sex.

I don't really want to go it into detail, but I'll give you an idea:

Sit in a therapist's office and watch boys and girls kiss, pet, and do it again and again. Then talk about it with the therapists, about what they are doing, and be forced to close your eyes and visualize doing this with someone in your class—again and again.

Then sit in a therapist's office and watch boys and boys and girls and girls interact and be forced to slap yourself with a ruler, or worse, because it was always really ugly if I showed signs of liking it. That's when they made me use the little taser thing on myself. They made me pick a spot where no one would notice the marks left behind. I usually picked the top inside portion of my thigh.

This made them very happy, I think because it was so close to my...never mind.

When we weren't in the office, I had to wear a rubber band around my wrist and snap it really hard every time I looked at another girl and thought something about her. Even if it was a simple thought, such as I liked her shirt or something like that. If I didn't have the snap marks to prove my efforts, then life at home got even uglier.

I remember thinking, forget about looking at other people. I needed to snap my wrists, just for the sake of leaving marks, so I didn't get punished even worse.

I don't want to get into this anymore. I think you get the idea. I've become one of those messed up people who have survived child sexual abuse.

Scratch that, I'm now one of those messed up people who lived through child sexual abuse.

You can't turn back time, but you can change the time that is yet to come.

Sincerely,
The Lost

9

Hope in the Balance

Hope in the Balance

The Girl waits in the trees, bound by agonizing patience, yearning to know the death of neglect and the protection from the force upon her shins. The gaze's circumference shows the madness cloaked over every nook and cranny.

Aberration invades every glance as the carriers choose to paralyze. She chooses to stay and begs for the delusion of candy. For without the comfort of madness, the Art would have order, and that, the children in the trees could never have.

Balanced on the wood, the pinched learn to toy with ropes.

With the letters of the stitch, the thread begins to fill the silk pages, and with every needle's pierce, it is shown the puncture of a Child's heart and the will to drink from the well of death.

Shaded by the Princess of Loveliness, the face of torture sits on every wrist, hiding the truth in mundane time. The longing to belong is now a road, which bellows from the depths of the wave's tomb. I seek to run from the only knowledge of love I have, which is what love is not. I seek to end every breath taken not beside her.

How I long to never dream again of someone missing, and for the time, which tortures my awakening with thoughts of this beautiful brutality finally ceasing.

It is the conditional love of nurturers, which condone the pillage of children, and arrange violation as a consequence to those who discover the truth about the earth's rotation.

Consideration of those we do not know can change the world.
Consideration of the person standing next to you can save humanity,
but only if you have the courage of your conviction.

"Stay right where you are, things around you are not as they
seem," the Casting Director calls, as the facade takes life and the
current of the wake parts the bay, where even the marshes are
beautiful, as the pelicans rest in its moss.

The power of the Butterfly's effect is not to be overlooked.
We think it is beasts like lions and bears, which are the threat.
But it is those who are blind to the delicate and vicious elegance of
the paper wings we must be wary of, for with one light flap of her
vibrant softness, she can cause hearts to weep,
and souls to be lost forever.

The symphony begins to warm in the chill.
Its notes strip the air from within my small body,
only to leave me gasping from the sound of lovely torture,
which is birthed from its harmony.

Hearts swell from fear, only to be calmed by the child's turnstile.
For it is the power of an innocent perspective,
which softly sleep at the ears of greatness,
who create the lens of the future,
that provide prevention to the persecuted,
who allow the grounded to jump,
that feed the ones who do not know fullness,
who define the colors and change with hope.

American Psychiatric Association
Sounds the Alarm

A 2014 report issued by the APA states the following: "Childhood psychological abuse is as harmful as sexual abuse."

APA data reveals that nearly three million U.S. children experience some form of psychological maltreatment annually, and that psychological maltreatment is "the most challenging and prevalent form of child abuse and neglect."

The APA concluded in this report that, "given the prevalence of childhood psychological abuse and severity of harm to young victims, it should be at the forefront of mental health and social service training."

Source: American Psychological Association, "Childhood Psychological Abuse as Harmful as Sexual or Physical Abuse," press release, October 8, 2014, http://www.apa.org/news/press/releases/2014/10/psychologi cal-abuse.aspx.

FROM: Child victim Of conversion therapy
TO: Minnesota State Legislature, U.S. Congress

May 25, 2018

Dear Elected Officials,

Greetings, honored men and women. My teachers wanted me to always be able to take care of myself and are tried to load me up with the skill sets to do so. Not all my memories are filled with horror, because there have been some really special moments created just for me at school. You know what? Some of those moments have saved my life, and I imagine those special memories will save my life at some time again in the future.

I remember the first time I went to a courthouse. It was for an elementary school trip. I stood behind the defendant's gate, and in that moment, I first hoped to get the honor of standing before the great lawmakers of this state and contribute to the beauty that is the law. Learning about the law was amazing to me, and learning, too, about what can be done. The gift of the law is like nothing else on this earth.

Our great governmental entities are you, its keepers. You have a grave weight on your back every day. I will always show the utmost respect to you lawmakers and keepers, for it is you who keep us safe.

But Madams and Sirs, I am disheartened. I fear I will not see my day in court. You see, I am going blind and deaf. I cannot hear anymore because the sound of a belt whipping against my body has made me go deaf.

Is this just?

I cannot see any more from all the times my head has

been held under water as punishment for my sexual orientation.

Is this just?

I cannot hear myself think any more from all the yelling in my face: "You are retarded, a disgusting idiot."

Is this just?

The counselors said I should eat only after the rest of my family has eaten, and only if for some reason my presence is requested at the dinner table, usually to save face in front of company. Then, I am allowed to speak, but only when spoken to.

Is this just?

The counselors think I should draw an X over my heart and wear it under my shirt so I know where to put the gun if I look at another girl.

Is this just?

The counselors think I should put needles in my fingertips every time I think about wanting to kiss a girl.

Is this just?

The counselors think I should put on my stone-washed jeans and stand in front of a mirror and tell myself I am worthless and ugly for 30 minutes a day. Then, they think I should put on my dress and stand in front of a mirror and tell myself I am "pretty in pink."

Is this just?

I want to be a lawyer, but first I need the law to fight for me. I suppose I am asking for a present from the Keepers of the Law.

Sincerely,
Biding My Time

10

Shadows Of Love

Shadows Of Love

Today the puzzle pieces seemed all jumbled.
In the backdrops of the pictures sits the scenery of the future.
The gentle brush of the ice on the nightlight's caged heart,
awaits in the nursery rhymes.
In the backdrops of the pictures sits What should have been.
Look closely, or risk the loneliness of continued darkness
for times to come.

See the love in the moments of blindness, hiding in the corner.
The Shadow guides us to follow the reflections of love,
traveling at our feet.
The Shadow turns our heads when the travel is misguided.
The Shadow casts the leap of faith in the close at hand with the
glimpse of side-by-side

The other night I dreamt I ran to the arch you built.
It was beautiful, but sad, because your smile was not there.

Once upon a time, suddenly the day went dark.
A day without color is like the vicious bite of the white wind
against my cheek, leaving the blood frozen in a smile.
A day without music is the deafening sight of a child
without the courage to laugh.

I love you more than anything, the Shadow whispers to his son.
Close your eyes, and blindly trust the voices to reconstruct the
universe for you, a Shadow whispers to his daughter.
Look around yourself and realize everything has meaning,
the Arts require.

Walk in the darkness, to find the light, the questions pose?
Piece together the jigsaw, Everest tasks.

Find a voice for the fisherman's pain evident in the gills torture, the silenced Artist reflects from the ocean's silver bottom.

Today, the Shadow's love was in the lap of bay & flap of the gull.

Today, the Shadow's love was in the feeling of safety in the quiet streets.

Today, the Shadow's love became a careless moment dancing in the aisles.

Today, the sacrifice of the silent Shadow is the song of devotion, which whispers to us from the doorway...First I loved you from the shadows, now I love you from the light. I am so proud of you.

Multiple Factors Create Abuse

The World Health Organization and the International Society for Prevention of Child Abuse and Neglect identify multiple factors at the level of the individual, their relationships, their local community, and their society at large that combine to influence the occurrence of child maltreatment. At the individual level, such factors include age, sex, and personal history, while at the level of society, factors contributing to child maltreatment include cultural norms encouraging harsh physical punishment of children, economic inequality, and the lack of social safety nets.

Source: World Health Organization and International Society for Prevention of Child Abuse and Neglect, "The Nature and Consequences of Child Maltreatment," chap. 1, in *Preventing Child Maltreatment: A Guide to Taking Action and Generating Evidence* (Geneva: World Health Organization Press, 2006).

FROM: Child victim Of conversion therapy
TO: Whom this should concern

May 11, 2018

Dear Mom and Dad,

I don't know what to say. You never even gave me a shot, to be okay at life. You took away my shot at being normal, you know? I ask myself a lot, why didn't you talk to me about what you were thinking and feeling? Why didn't you say, "I'm afraid for you." Why didn't you just look at me and say, "I don't understand you." Maybe we could have talked at little, instead of creating this talk-less state.

I guess I have a lot of questions, but I'm not sure you have the courage to answer them. If you do, you will follow your gut and know that this is *your child* writing this letter to you. I know there is conviction within you, because I know on some level you both survived your own oppression and conversion at the hands of your parents and society. I know you have conviction because without it you could not sleep at night.

I just do not know if you have courage. Your response to this letter will tell me. If you have courage, you will open my bedroom door and talk to me.

I want you to know that if you harness the courage I know is in you, I will not reject you. But you must say, "You are my child, and I do love you."

I do not understand why you feel the way you do. If you can come to me and say "I do not understand," then I will not reject you. Learning about people who are "different" is always a little uncomfortable. Usually, the beauty about it all in the end is that we are all connected, and a sum of our parts and usually our diversity is what makes us a great team.

The truth is, I will always be who I am, and I have always been who I was, and I will never be anything different than what I am made of.

The truth is, that can or cannot include being your child. Who I am is not a choice, unlike your decided parenthood. Just keep in mind I did not choose to be your child, but you did choose to have me.

I ask you, do you have the courage of your convictions to be the parent you intended to be? Or, are you a weak link in the animal chain that abandons their offspring and corrupts the cycle of life?

Do not forget, your private acknowledgement of my sexuality began well before I was 10 years old. This is your admittance that my sexuality is in fact inherent, and genetic. Do not be misled by the lies of leaders who tell you they can change the genetics within me. This is, quite frankly, obtuse.

For your own dignity, I ask you to rise above the stupidity and come through my bedroom door and sit next to me and say, "I do not understand why you feel the way you feel, and it is hard for me, and I do not know how to be around you sometimes, but I want to be there for you always, more than anything."

Please come through my bedroom door in realization that all we have is now, and each other. Please realize that those you seek social approval from, when death is the face before you, are not more important than my life, the life you created.

To the parents of my friends: Please walk through your child's bedroom doors and talk to them. While I respect you more than my own parents, your silence is detrimental. By not going through your child's bedroom door and asking, "Do you like boys or girls?" you are rejecting them.

Your silence perpetuates their silence, and regardless of the answer, they need to talk about their thoughts and feelings about boys and girls.

Silence is deadly, as we all know.

"It was when we said nothing at all that millions of the 'different' were massacred."

To the parents of my friends: Do not be afraid.

I know you will always be there and love your children. That is why you look at me with love. Please open your children's bedroom doors and ask. I promise it will be okay, but it is time to face the beautiful truths and stop holding your breath.

Mom and Dad, please come through my bedroom door and talk to me.

Sincerely,
Your child

11
The Beautiful

The Beautiful

With the Chants of hate goes the liberty of humanity,
Doors become meaningless and what was once private,
become public games.

There in the streets, where the school children traveled,
lie the dead bodies draped over the crosswalks.

The Mastress in the sky paints the plane Blue Green
The Board converges as their shadow emerges from the lion's den.
Survival would be harnessing the strength to be empowered to be
unaffected

Upon the 13th step I sat, my feathers now ready for flight.
Hell and horror once a dream, only to bring flight and fury to the
future's firm.

From A-Z, flight to sea, the walk to Way, the drudge to J. &
A., bare to B, born to free, blue suede, black capes, and red
dances.

The terror in truth and being torn through time…from Blind to
Hitchcock and all the stories the Nights
could Paint.

From deaf, to the Dress circle at Madam Butterfly, conducted by
the Symphony.

From paralyzed to the march of many and dancing in the Park.

From Flags of Rubles to Windows full of Whispers.

From crumbling Buildings to buildings of Puzzles in the sky,

From silence to the glorious sound of the trumpets played by statues around the World,

From unknown love down under, to the sound of "Same Love,"

From picture Frames to reflections in window frames of Women in yellow dresses,

From pins and needles to the Pins Interest,

From pound puppies to passing puppies on the way to yoga,

From gunshots and brick walls to Butterflies and Violins,

From the voice when I did not have one that led to the left,

From bleakness to the stars target of love,

From the depths of danger to knowing that the birds were sent to my window sills,

From unknown skies to the bluebird's eye in the sky,

From the brutality of bobby pins to forever safety with musicians waving from the bus,

From soil to space,

From football games to walking by the zebras on the street who love to look for the lavender flower,

From laughless to the SignS laughter out loud,

From frozen with fear to window anchors of her & me and U and W.i,

From lost bunnies to pink bunnies that keep on going back and forth to the board walk to "check,."

From the upside-down Mermaid to the left side up class room,

From nowhere to there to here, and hopefully soon to be home again in the Beyond,

From the neglected subway rats to Mosaics and matching patterns on building tops,

From the base of the Congo with the Rhinoceros, to the Rose Gold Bullets of Vengeance, Time, and Daughters,

From soil to space,

From the Voice when I did not have one that led to the left,

From the depths of danger to knowing that love is right here sitting on my window sill,

I tell the tale of a story from ancient to adolescent...

I tell the tale of an ugly, beautiful.

Suicidal Ideation and Attempts Among Students in Grades 8, 10, and 12—Utah, 2015

Marissa L. Zwald et al.

Suicidal thoughts and behaviors among youths are important public health concerns in Utah, where the suicide rate among youths consistently exceeds the national rate and has been increasing for nearly a decade. In March, 2017, CDC was invited to assist the Utah Department of Health (UDOH) with an investigation to characterize the epidemiology of fatal and nonfatal suicidal behaviors and identify risk and protective factors associated with these behaviors, among youths aged 10–17 years. This report presents findings related to nonfatal suicidal behaviors among Utah youths. Among 27,329 respondents in grades 8, 10, and 12, 19.6% reported suicidal ideation and 8.2% reported suicide attempts in the preceding 12 months. Significant risk factors for suicidal ideation and attempts included being bullied, illegal substance use in the previous month, and psychological distress.

A significant protective factor for suicidal ideation and attempts was a supportive family environment.

Source: Marissa L. Zwald et al., "**Suicidal Ideation and Attempts Among Students in Grades 8, 10, and 12—Utah, 2015,**" *Morbidity and Mortality Weekly Report*, **April 20, 2018,** https://www.hsdl.org/?view&did=809589.

FROM: Child victim Of conversion therapy
TO: Utah State Legislature, U.S. Congress

January 21, 2018

Dear Elected Officials,

I am kept pretty isolated, so I don't know what it's like in the towns I see on TV. I am told that not all homes are like mine, that there are parents out there who don't send their kids to the doctors I have to go to. I am told there are parents who don't make their children bleed or burn because they like to swing with other boys.

One night, I was just sitting here thinking I should just do what my parents want me to do and jump in front of one of them damn trucks on the interstate. Maybe I am a piece of "you know what" that deserves all the pain the doctors make me go through.

I was thinking, I just can't take it no more. I just don't think my lungs can take one more punch. I just don't think my toes can bear the bleach no more. Mama said she was gonna use the iron next time I looked at a boy side- ways. I hate that thing. It hurts for days. But Mama says that's why the doctors tell her to use it on me, because I remember for days what I did wrong.

I know I'm different. I know that I ain't like other boys. But I'm pretty smart. Did you know that if you are kind to people they are more likely to be kind to you? You know how I know that? I tried it, and it worked. You know something else? Did you know that when you are really scared and in a lot of pain, if you tell yourself in your mind, "It doesn't hurt," you can make the pain go away.

One night, I called this Help Hotline for Kids in

Crisis. I just talked to this real smart lady on the phone, and she told me that the mind is a very powerful tool, and I am learning to harness the power of my mind. After I talked to this lady I thought, well, maybe I do have some smarts. She also told me that not all homes are like mine, but that some homes are like mine.

I told her that my friend down the way got taken to the hospital when he got hurt playing, and the nurses thought maybe his parents were hurting him, but that wasn't the case. Then I told this lady that I was scared of being hurt and asked her if the law thought that was okay, and you know what? The law thinks it *is* okay.

I know I don't know much, but that don't seem to make no sense to me.

Now I got a bigger problem.

Remember that boy I told you about, the one from down the way? He has this friend, and one day, at the end of the school, he brought his papa's gun in his bag to school. I walked into that bathroom and he was showing it off.

He pointed that thing right at me and called me the "F" word and said if I told anyone he'd shoot me, just like those kids at the other schools on the news. He told me that it was because of kids like me that we have to "fire away" at schools.

I just don't understand any of this.

Kids are being shot in school. Kids are being beaten at home, and kids are dying by the trucks that pass by, and meanwhile, the laws in the United States of America—and the people who make them—aren't doing everything they can to stop all these things from happening.

Why not?

I don't know much, but I know this. I am gonna die young, that's for certain. I'm either gonna get shot up at school, beaten to death by my parents because the therapists told them to, or I'm gone get myself run over because I just can't take it no more.

I'll tell you what, these odds ain't good. All because I like to swing with boys. Crazy. Just crazy.

Sincerely,
The Walking Dead

"There Has Been, on Average, One School Shooting Ever Week This Year,"

Saeed Ahmed and Christina Walker

CNN, May 25, 2018,

https://www/cnn.com/2018/03/02/us/school-schootings-2018-list-trnd/index.html.

12

The Chef & the Moon Walker

The Chef & the Moon Walker

1 — The Restaurant

"Come child," the Arts sound, as they float about their stage, offering instructions to save my life.

Down the rabbit hole we went, to merge the people's structure and see the color purple for the first time. For it was when she showed me the beauty of the color of African skin that one of the great wonders of the world was unlocked to me.

It is then I learned of the discomfort of ambiance.
The instinct to avoid a glance dims my dining room.
The reality of racial tension in this world remains in the lights, which shade our dining rooms in restaurants across the world.

Our struggle to understand our individual sexuality strikes my Guest's ears just before appetizers.

The sharp edges of the bar are ever so slightly dulled by the Mixologist's shake and the Guests smile while they unknowingly enjoy the children's music and moisten their lips with the cocktails that toil with their gender.

The cultural bridge nurtures the Guest as the somber or sexy interpretation of the song determines what will happen after they dine. All the while, the Director holds the worry that the political positioning of the tables will not go un-noticed.

The waiver of the dessert menu reminds us all just how steep the cultural taste buds are which we seek to bring together.

But oh, how sweet it is when they stay for the Piano Man, played by the Violist.

The hardship of our economic war is cut with the tender blade of a crumber, as the check is paid.

Oh, how I love it when the Guest's do not notice me as I wish them well. For it is only when they do not hear goodbye that I know they will be back. Because in that moment, all they can hear is the music, all they can feel is the warmth, all they can see are the colors.

It is when they do not say goodbye, that I know they will enjoy the rest of their evening. It is when they do not say goodbye that I can see the Grey cloaked around their shoulders.

I never knew the anguish of a dagger plunged through my heart until I saw the community tiptoe into my restaurant. For it is the uncertainty they would not be welcomed that allowed me to recognize the social divides which oppress our culture.

My hope for the world is that they will know the pleasure of tiptoeing through the turnstile after they have enjoyed their dining experience.

●

Dear Student,

The Master Chefs do not cook for the love of cooking.
We prepare nourishment for the love of people.
Now, I bow my head to your heart and hope my fingertips are gentle upon your bruised soul. I hope you hear the whisper of my soft skin amongst the hateful echoes of time.
I hope our gaze blankets your bleeding wounds.
I hope the flames beneath my skillet do no harm to the children.

110

I hope the kiss of my spoon upon your back is cool and kind.
I hope the color of our sauce is purple and not burgundy.
I hope thine recipe book is fit for Future Generations.
I hope.
The Master Chefs

Dear Master Chefs,

I hope you know I see the agony in your eyes when your laced
fingers rock me to sleep.
I hope you know I see the anguish you attempt to bear for us at
the triangles point.
I hope you know the path, which you have laid for us, is safe.
I hope you know that you feed the world not by fork and knife.
I hope you know you have taught the world to feed by fingertip.
I hope you know the Historian Chef is on his way, because of you.
Now, I bow my head to both of your hearts, and rest in the hope
which you have planted for me.

Your Student

●

2 — Outer Space

"Where are you from?" The Moon Walker wonders.

"The Future," the yielding whispers.

The Strong Arm pries: "What is it like?"

The limbs of Willow whispers: "Nourishment is not a tool of
persecution in the future. The Master of the Menu creates the
dreams of painted plates of joy and togetherness.

In the future, the Colors of Culture are worshiped for the living art they are.
In the future, the Dark Poet is honored for his Genuine Nature.
In the future, there is no need to call upon the Princess of Loveliness to sacrifice for the greater good.
In the future, nurture follows the lead of the Fathers of the Bell Tower.
In the future, a lift on the rising walls is a shared smile, instead of gut-wrenching sadness.
In the future, the Street Warriors are commended for bearing the puncture of the bald beast's claws.
In the future, the Wind of Dylan is heard by all and the gridlines of segregation are blurred, leaving the melting pot of greatness to flourish as the Founding Fathers intended.
In the future, We the People are for the persons passing by.
In the future, children do not cry in the corner because they've learned that hate lives down the hall.
In the future, the great divide does not exist.
In the future, the innocent march each day to the beat of the Constitution in their blood.

In the future, we learn from the lens removed by THE DIRECTOR, and heed the sorrow of humanity's song upon set and stage.

In the future, United We Stand and Live in the Love of Light's Beyond.
In the future, hope lives in the eyes of the children.
In the future, freedom is heartfelt, irrefutable and awe inspiring.
In the future, the cloth of brotherly love is worn by all.
Because in the future…the world is tidensoui…

In a moment of advocacy, the Moon Walker removes the helmet and gasps, as the air of the future fills her heart with hope.

The Hero of Change looks at the child of destiny, and with a smile of relief asks, "May I hold your hand?"

In the comfort of the Hero's clasp the humble divulges, "I am scared the world won't be able to learn to breath without their helmets."

"They will," the Hero says, with calming assurance. "We will hold their hands and waive the world with a chain of change."

Dear Legislator

13

A Call to Action

CALL TO ACTION
#WriteToFight

There are currently 36 states without laws prohibiting licensed mental health professionals from practicing conversion therapy techniques on minors

The following states currently *have* laws forbidding the practice of conversion therapy on minors: California, Connecticut, New Jersey, Delaware, Hawai'i, Oregon and Illinois, Maryland, Vermont, Nevada, New Hampshire, New Mexico, and Rhode Island, Washington and Washington, D.C. and New York.

Please write to your state, local, federal and Presidential representatives to advocate for the implementation of laws which prohibit conversion therapy practices on minors in all the states still without protective laws.

Please feel free to use the information provided, in the content of your letter and/or email, as a guide to express the need for laws that prohibit conversion therapy practices in America. Remember, this is a legal issue, and it is important we communicate with knowledge and discernment in order to *not* be dismissed anymore.

This is an urgent issue of stopping child abuse from continuing to be permitted in America. Thank you for listening to the voices of those effected by conversion therapy. You are power. It is time to be empowered to write to fight for what is right.

Thank you for your time,
Vellah Jones and the Children's Committee

CALL TO ACTION
#WriteToFight

Please visit
WWW.dearcongress.LOVE
to #WriteToFight

Here you will find the playbook for action.

All links on the website are provided so you can easily find emails, phone numbers, and addresses for all State and Federal Elected officials, as well as the President of the United States.

With the links on WWW.dearcongress.LOVE you can send your letters and emails, advocating for the implementation of laws, preventing conversion therapy practices on minors in the United States of America.

WRITE TO FIGHT FOR WHAT IS RIGHT!!!
"We can change the world with words."
Maya Angelou

<u>CALL TO ACTION</u>
#WriteToFight

WRITE TO FIGHT FOR WHAT IS RIGHT!!!

Dearest Writers:

What you have to say is important. Always write what your heart tells you. Speak to your reader with knowledge and discernment. If you so desire, or need to, please feel free to use the letter on the next page as a template when writing your elected officials, requiring they implement laws which prohibit conversion therapy practices on minors in America.

We have a responsibility. Now…it's time to save some lives!

Thank you for your time,
Vellah Jones

Dear Elected Officials,

I would like to bring to your attention, an issue of child rights, which are currently being neglected and are at risk in the state of _____ (input state).

Incidents of licensed mental health professionals using conversion therapy techniques on American children is rising to alarming levels, and it is growing.

Damages resulting from conversion therapy, which organizations such as the APA, American Academy of Child Adolescent Psychiatry, American Academy of Pediatrics, American Association of Marriage and Family Therapy, American College of Physicians, American Counseling Association, American Medical Association, American School Counselor Association, American School Health Association, National School of Social Workers PAN American Health Organization, and many other accredited institutions have confirmed to be unfounded and harmful, are negatively impacting the physical, psychological, and emotional development of individuals at a highly detrimental rate.

Conversion therapy is a compilation of "therapeutic" techniques that all fall under the category of child abuse according to the World Health Organization, Centers for Disease Control, APA and the Child Abuse Prevention and Treatment Act. Conversion therapy also often includes the types of psychological and physical abuse familiar to abused children not subjected to conversion therapy. These types of abuse include, but are not limited to:

➢ Coercing suicide and suicidal role play in an effort to encourage the act of suicide

➢ Forced exposure to heterosexual behavior in visual, verbal and actual forms

➢ Various forms of corporal punishment including, but not limited to: hitting, slapping, punching, burning, poking and pinching

➢ Coercing self-harm including snapping a rubber band around the left wrist

➢ Verbal abuse including name calling and negative labeling

➢ Neglect including deliberately with holding physical and verbal affection necessary for adequate development

➢ Electro shock therapy

➢ Coercing self-mutilation in the form of using a needle to damage and peel off one's skin

➢ Hypnosis in an effort to brain wash

➢ The use of drugs to induce incoherence and immobilization

➢ Orgasmic reconditioning

Currently there are 15 states with laws preventing the practice of conversion therapy in an effort to change someone's sexual orientation or gender identity. Each of these states provide a model for how other states can initiate to protect Americans and abolish conversion therapy as an active practice in the United States.

I hope you will be inspired by their decisions and take appropriate action in your state. If we all dedicate our efforts to positive change, our country can become a safer and healthier place for everyone.

Sincerely,
A Concerned Citizen Who Votes

CALL TO ACTION
#WriteToFight

WRITE TO FIGHT FOR WHAT IS RIGHT!

What Else Can You Do?

Besides writing your State and Federal elected officials please participate in the #WriteToFight and #BornPerfect campaigns now underway on social media.

Please stay tuned on **www.dearcongress.love** and sign up for the WriteToFight blog to receive updates on the following:

The Children's Committee

Calls to Action

The Voices

Important information on upcoming events

Get connected with organizations across the country that believe in the mission

Information about a new TV series currently in development that dive into the web of conversion therapy

To share your personal story with Vellah Jones.

CALL TO ACTION
#WriteToFight

To find additional resources, for those who wish to become more involved and/or to refer someone who is currently being abused by conversion therapy, please visit:

#BornPerfect: The Campaign to End Conversion Therapy

National Center for Lesbian Rights
NCLRights.org

WWW.dearcongress.love

Human Rights Campaign
Hrc.org

To find your local LGBTQ center please visit:
WWW.lgbtcenters.org

Laws Preventing Conversion Therapy for Minors Under Age 18 Still Lacking in 37 States
Source: Human Rights Watch

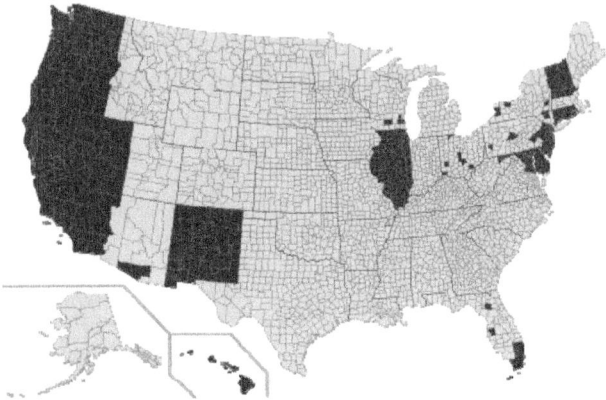

U.S. cities and counties with bans on conversion therapy for minors on the basis of sexual orientation and gender identity appear dark. The rest of the country still allows it.

ACKNOWLEDGMENTS

Dearest Arts and Angels,

If ever you wondered if you make a difference, if ever you wondered if this is all only about superficial non-sense, please know, that in the truth only your whisper has the power. For the facade is nothing compared to the power of your script or stage or screen or words or Lights or sculptures or fabrics or jewels and stones and rocks or instruments or humor on the walls or characters on the streets or fortune cookies or parades of powerful love & safety or sirens or strokes or sea glass or movements or colors or buildings or pavements or journey & journal   or the edge which you challenge the world with.

Every time you question, "Do I believe," know that means you are on the right path.

Thank you for my reflection...for when I look, it is not the hate which I see...it is your truths which I know...I just wanted you to know...U are the May in February, you are every CLOUD I look at, you are The Sun & the moon & the trees; you are a gift to the world, you are the green of grass and blue of the sky and Stars in daylight...you are the eye contact in the darkness...you are the givers of my life and the Voice when ! did not have one.

Forever and Always,

A Believer

Dearest David,

I am not sure what forces of the universe brought us together, but I am certain I will forever be in your debt as a result.

Did you ever meet someone and realize that the world is not what you thought it was because you learned of who they are? When darkness was all I knew...you were one of the ones, there with light.

David...in kindness you said to me, "This can never happen to you again." That was the first time I ever heard those words. I suppose it is like hearing the words, "you are free" for the first time. That moment means more to me, then you will ever know.

Thank you will never do justice to the contributions you have made to my life, and to the world.

Forever and Always,

Your Loving Friend

Dearest Readers,

Conviction in the moment is the courage, which changes the world and it is who you are. I am in awe of your conviction to read these stories. Know that I see the rare courage it has taken to get through these pages....and while it may seem small to you, please know the courage it took you to read these pages is profound...what you have done is profound.

Each and every one of you is awe-inspiring to me. I am so grateful. Whether you realize it or not, you all were with us on this journey...it is you who helped write this book. It is you, the readers of today and writers of tomorrow, who listened when the children of these stories needed it the most.

I feel sorrow for the imperfections of the world, but please know it is you, the readers of these pages, who are the art of life, of my life...you are the writers of the fight, without even knowing it.

I thank you for helping me define the truth of pricelessness, for showing me the unconditional.

Please know the position of your feet matter, please know you matter. What you do, what we have done matters, what we will do matters. You matter .... you are matter...the undefinable is defined in your actions....and I hope, in what you choose to do.

Thank you for your time,

The Love

ABOUT THE AUTHOR

VELLAH JONES knows first-hand the immediate and long-term effects of conversion therapy. This book is her first public effort to shine a light on the horrors of this practice and to affect positive legislative change in the land she loves and believes in—the United States of America.

Please visit WWW.dearcongress.LOVE

To the love of the sun, the moon, the night and the words,
To the love of the fire, ash, the air and the clouds,
You are my poetry's heartbeat

...

Printed in Great Britain
by Amazon